STARS OF THE NFL

By Tyler Blue

Abbeville Kids
An Imprint of Abbeville Press
New York London

Statistics are current as of March 24, 2023.

Please note: This book has not been authorized by the NFL.

Project editor: Lauren Orthey
Copy editor: Ashley Benning
Layout: Marina Drukman
Production director: Louise Kurtz

PHOTOGRAPHY CREDITS

Adobe Stock: front cover background (AStakhiv); pp. 2–3 (efks); pp. 4–5 (MT-R)

Alamy: p. 15 (Kirby Lee)

Icon Sportswire: p. 7 (Scott W. Grau); p. 9 (Jordon Kelly); p. 11 (Nicole Fridling); p. 13 and front cover left (Douglas Stringer); p. 17 and back cover (Randy Litzinger); p. 19 (Robin Alam); p. 21 (Brian Rothmuller); pp. 23, 25 (Peter Joneleit); p. 27 (Bryan Lynn); p. 29 and back cover (Andy Lewis); p. 31 (Frank Jansky); p. 33 (Michael Allio); p. 35 and front cover right (Nick Wosika); pp. 37, 39 (Andy Lewis); p. 41 (Rich von Biber-stein); p. 43 (Rich Graessle); p. 45 and front cover middle (Cliff Welch); p. 47 (Michael Allio); p. 49 (Andy Lewis); p. 51 (Charles Brock); p. 53 and back cover (Frank Jansky); p. 55 (David Rosenblum); p. 57 (Charles Brock); p. 59 (Jeffrey Brown); p. 61 (Robin Alam); pp. 62–63 (Andy Lewis)

First edition
10 9 8 7 6 5 4 3 2

ISBN 978-0-7892-1457-7

Library of Congress Cataloging-in-Publication Data available upon request

For bulk and premium sales and for text adoption procedures, write to Customer Service Manager, Abbeville Press, 655 Third Avenue, New York, NY 10017, or call 1-800-Artbook.

Visit Abbeville Kids online at www.abbevillefamily.com.

CONTENTS

Josh Allen

After his freshman year at Reedley Junior College, Josh Allen sent an email to more than 1,000 Division I coaches, imploring them to take a look at his highlight video and give him a chance to be their quarterback. The unsolicited emails ultimately led to just one scholarship offer—from the University of Wyoming, not exactly the cream of the college football crop. But at least it was something. Coming out of high school, not a single D-I program wanted Allen, who, 10 years later, is a two-time Pro Bowler for the Buffalo Bills.

How could it be that one of the most dynamic quarterbacks in the NFL was once the most overlooked quarterback in the country? A large part of the answer stems from where Josh grew up: in the tiny town of Firebaugh in California's Central Valley. With a population of about 8,000, Firebaugh is a bit off the beaten path. It is known more for its produce than for producing highly talented athletes.

Allen's great-grandfather, an immigrant from Sweden, somehow landed in Firebaugh during the Great Depression. Allen's grandfather established a family farm in 1975—now run by Josh's father Joel. Josh learned how to work hard by watching his father, who would often head out to the fields before the sun rose and not return until after it had set. Josh pitched in where needed, be it weeding fields, driving a tractor, or moving irrigation pipe. When he wasn't on the farm, he often bused tables at The Farmer's Daughter, a restaurant his mom Lavonne ran.

On top of that, Josh participated in just about every sport imaginable, including baseball, basketball, football, golf, karate, and swimming.

That didn't leave him much time to attend the prestigious passing camps that other quarterbacks with D-I aspirations so often do. Josh did have an opportunity to transfer to a larger high school that would have afforded him greater exposure, but he chose to stick with Firebaugh, staying true to the family mantra: You bloom where you're planted.

And so it was that Allen's dream of playing big-time college football came down to Wyoming. Head coach Craig Bohl was the only D-I coach to visit Allen at his home, telling him that Wyoming wanted to make him the face of the program. Allen committed and got a chance to play in the first game of the 2015 season, but broke his collarbone 13 plays into his tenure.

That injury, though, gave him the chance to really learn the offense and focus on gaining strength, speed, and agility. In 2016, he threw for over 3,000 yards and 28 touchdowns. His numbers and measurables—by this time Allen was 6'5" and about 230 pounds—made him think about turning professional early. But he decided he needed one more year of college, and following the 2017 season he was considered one of the top quarterback prospects in his class.

Buffalo drafted him with the seventh pick in 2018. After a couple of so-so years, Allen took the NFL by storm in 2020, throwing for 4,544 yards and 37 TDs while completing an outstanding 69.2% of his attempts. He put up similar numbers the next two years, cementing himself as one of the premier quarterbacks in the league. Nobody is overlooking Josh Allen anymore.

Position: **Quarterback**
Hometown: **Firebaugh, CA**
Born: **May 21, 1996**
Height: **6'5"**
Weight: **237 lb.**
Team: **Buffalo Bills**
Career Passing TDs: **138**

Budda Baker

When Bishard Baker was an infant, his mother Michelle thought his big, round belly made him look like a little Buddha doll. And so now, while very few people are aware of who Bishard Baker is, for millions of football fans across the country, Budda Baker is a household name.

The Arizona Cardinals drafted Baker in the second round of the 2017 draft after the Bellevue, Washington, native's stellar three-year career at the University of Washington. Since then, Baker has only continued to excel. In his six years in the NFL, the hard-hitting dynamo has made up for his relative lack of size (he's only 5'10") with his explosive athleticism. He's earned five Pro Bowl appearances and been named a first-team All-Pro twice.

If Baker looks angry out on the field, it's because he is. To understand the source of that anger, one must first know the story of Budda's older brother Robert.

Budda was 13 years old when he lost his brother for the first time. Robert got caught up with the wrong crowd and was sentenced to eight years in prison after being charged with first-degree robbery and possession of a firearm. As he left the courthouse that day, Robert asked his escorting officers to remove his belt and hand it to Budda. The message was clear: Budda was the man of the house now.

Budda relished the role, taking care of his mother who was battling several health issues and looking after his four sisters. Through it all, his bond with Robert somehow grew. The two wrote letters to each other, which Budda would pin to the wall of his bedroom. They talked on the phone every other week, and Budda visited his brother monthly.

During this time, Budda was growing from an annoying little brother into a legitimate NFL prospect. In prison, Robert caught as many Washington Huskies games as he could, cheering wildly whenever his brother appeared on-screen. Then, in November 2016, Robert became a free man once again, out early on a work-release program. On November 12 of that year, Robert finally got to see his little brother play in person. They were reunited; all was right again.

Until April 22, 2018.

In the early hours of that morning outside a club in Seattle, Robert Baker was shot and killed for reasons unknown. Budda had lost his brother once more—this time for good. Baker felt almost debilitating pain, but decided he wouldn't let that pain ruin him. Instead, it motivates him to give everything he has out on the field. In other words, Budda Baker makes his NFL opponents feel his pain.

Position: **Free Safety**
Hometown: **Bellevue, WA**
Born: **Jan. 10, 1996**
Height: **5'10"**
Weight: **195 lb.**
Team: **Arizona Cardinals**
Career Interceptions: **7**

Saquon Barkley

Alibay Barkley, father of New York Giants star running back Saquon, knew his son had a thing for football early on. One day, when three-year-old Saquon was watching a New York Jets game with Alibay in their Bronx, New York, home, he pointed at Jets running back Curtis Martin and said, "When I grow up, I'm going to be No. 28."

That bold prediction proved quite prescient. Though he may not be No. 28 for the New York Jets, Saquon Barkley is No. 26 for the New York Giants, after the team selected Barkley with the No. 2 pick of the 2018 NFL draft following a stellar career at Pennsylvania State University.

Barkley burst onto the scene in his inaugural year with the Giants, earning Offensive Rookie of the Year honors after rushing for 1,307 yards and 11 touchdowns while adding another 721 yards and four touchdowns through the air. Injuries threatened to derail his career over the next three seasons, but Barkley returned to form in 2022, making his second Pro Bowl team and reestablishing himself as one of the NFL's brightest young stars.

Athleticism runs in Saquon's family. His father was a Golden Glove boxer whose career was cut short by some bad personal decisions and a shoulder injury. Alibay's uncle, Iran Barkley, was a three-time middleweight boxing world champion. Saquon himself is built like a tank but moves like a Ferrari. He is officially listed at 5'11" and 233 pounds. He squats 650 pounds and yet is explosive enough to power clean 405 pounds and run the 40-yard dash in 4.4 seconds. No wonder defenses find it so difficult to tackle him.

Though born in the Bronx, Saquon spent much of his childhood growing up in rural Pennsylvania. His mother Tonya Johnson thought her family could use a change of scenery as trouble always seemed to find Alibay in New York. Though at first reluctant, Alibay finally relented, and the family moved to Bethlehem, Pennsylvania, where Johnson had relatives, in 2001.

After a couple of moves, Saquon's family eventually settled in Coplay, Pennsylvania, a close-knit town of just 3,500. As an undersized freshman at Whitehall High School, Barkley considered giving up on football altogether. But his father, who always felt he had given up too easily on his boxing aspirations, encouraged his son to stick it out. Saquon listened—and blossomed, becoming a highly recruited player who would be a legend at Penn State for his highlight-reel runs and weight-room feats.

That perseverance paid off in his professional career after Barkley tore his ACL in the second week of the 2020 season. He rehabbed relentlessly, and his successful 2022 campaign proved all that hard work was worth it.

Position: **Running Back**
Hometown: **Bronx, NY**
Born: **Feb. 9, 1997**
Height: **5'11"**
Weight: **233 lb.**
Team: **New York Giants**
Career Rushing Yards: **4,249**

Nick Bosa

When John and Cheryl Bosa told their seven-year-old son Nick that he couldn't play football yet, Nick threw an epic tantrum, informing his parents he would die if he didn't get to play. The parents had a decision to make: Stand their ground or give in to their son. San Francisco 49ers defensive end Nick Bosa began playing football that year.

The 2022 NFL Defensive Player of the Year knew exactly what kind of football player he wanted to be right from the start. During his first-ever practice, Cheryl watched as her youngest son walked right up to the coach and engaged him in a conversation. After a while, the coach nodded and pointed in a direction that Nick immediately sprang toward. Cheryl later found out the coach initially had Nick playing offense, but Nick politely explained to him that he was meant for defense. Once again, he got his way.

That Nick Bosa even then prioritized sacks over touchdowns probably shouldn't come as much of a surprise. It's literally in his blood. John played defensive end in the NFL as well, becoming a first round pick for the Miami Dolphins in 1987. Nick's older brother Joey followed in his father's footsteps and was the third player selected in the 2016 NFL draft. When the 49ers took Nick with the second overall pick in 2019, the Bosas became the first family in NFL history to have three defensive linemen picked in the first round.

The Brothers Bosa–Joey calls himself Big Bear while Nick calls himself Little Bear–obviously are both extremely talented football players, but Nick had the benefit of learning from Joey, copying his every move–almost literally. Joey played three years at Ohio State before turning pro; Nick played three years at Ohio State before turning pro. Joey was the 2016 Defensive Rookie of the Year; Nick was the 2019 Defensive Rookie of the Year. Both brothers wear No. 97, the same number as their father.

Growing up, everything the brothers did turned into a competition, which often ended in some sort of physical altercation. However, their relationship changed forever during the 2012 football season, when for the first and only time in their lives they were teammates. Nick earned a starting spot on the defensive line as a freshman at St. Thomas Aquinas High School alongside Joey, a senior. Together they helped the school win a state championship. It was then that the brothers also became best friends.

A football team often forms a brotherhood. For Nick and Joey, football forged a lasting friendship between brothers.

Position: **Defensive End**
Hometown: **Fort Lauderdale, FL**
Born: **Oct. 23, 1997**
Height: **6'4"**
Weight: **266 lb.**
Team: **San Francisco 49ers**
Career Sacks: **43.0**

Joe Burrow

The family of Cincinnati Bengals 26-year-old quarterback Joe Burrow has a history of producing star football players—defensive players, to be specific. His uncle played safety at Ole Miss in the 1980s, and Joe's father Jimmy was a defensive back at Nebraska. Joe's two brothers, Jamie and Dan, also played defense for the Cornhuskers. As if that weren't enough, Jimmy was a longtime college defensive coordinator as well.

So how, exactly, did Joe ever wind up on the offensive side of the game? Well, his third grade team didn't have anybody who could play quarterback, so head coach Jimmy inserted his son in the position. It turned out to be a pretty good decision.

That's not to say that the 2019 Heisman Trophy winner—who took the college football world by storm that year by leading Louisiana State University to an undefeated national championship season before becoming the No. 1 pick of the 2020 NFL draft—had a smooth ride to stardom. For a while, it looked like his NFL dream would never be realized.

Joe was born in Ames, Iowa, at a time when his father was coaching Ames High School. But Jimmy's career took him away from Iowa when Joe was four years old—first to Nebraska, then to North Dakota. Finally, Jimmy found some stability when Ohio University hired him as its defensive coordinator in 2005, a position he kept until 2018.

So Joe spent most of his formative years in the Buckeye State, where he led Athens High School to the state championship game as a senior. The four-star recruit committed to Ohio State, but a hand injury that required surgery dropped him deep down the Buckeyes' depth chart. After three years riding the bench, it became clear to Burrow that if he wanted to chase his NFL aspirations, he would have to do so elsewhere.

He decided to continue his college career at LSU, where he won over his teammates—and the fan base—with his gritty play. He earned a reputation as being one of the toughest quarterbacks in the game. This trait, no doubt, came from that family tradition of producing defensive-minded men. He led the Tigers to 10 wins his first year as the starter, but it was his senior year that cemented him as a legend.

That season, he led the nation in completion percentage (76.3%), passing yards (5,671), and touchdowns (a mind-blowing 60). LSU demolished Oklahoma 63–28 in the semifinal of the College Football Playoff before beating Clemson by a comfortable margin of 42–25 to stake its claim as one of the most dominant teams in NCAA history.

Burrow's winning ways have only continued in Cincinnati. After a knee injury ended his rookie year early, in 2021 Joe surprised all the experts by leading the Bengals to the franchise's first Super Bowl appearance since the 1988 season. In 2022, Cincinnati came one game short of a second-straight Super Bowl, and Burrow made his first Pro Bowl team. More important, he made it clear that as long as he is around, the Bengals would be championship contenders.

Position: **Quarterback**
Hometown: **Ames, IA**
Born: **Dec. 10, 1996**
Height: **6'4"**
Weight: **221 lb.**
Team: **Cincinnati Bengals**
Career Completion Percentage: **68.2%**

Ja'Marr Chase

After the Cincinnati Bengals selected wide receiver Ja'Marr Chase with the fifth overall pick of the 2021 NFL draft, the Harvey, Louisiana, native knew just where he wanted to live—right next door to Bengals quarterback, and Chase's best friend, Joe Burrow. So Chase went to Burrow's street and knocked on every door, offering to buy each house until he found a taker. Now, the two Pro Bowlers and good pals are neighbors.

Chase had good reason to be so enthusiastic about teaming up with Burrow again. The first time the pair shared the same field as college teammates at Louisiana State University in 2019, they put together one of the most prolific seasons in NCAA football history. That year, Chase had 1,780 receiving yards and 20 touchdowns, both of which were Southeastern Conference records at the time but have since been broken.

More importantly, the Tigers went undefeated and won the National Championship. In LSU's title game victory against Clemson, Chase caught nine balls for 221 yards and two touchdowns. While Burrow took home the Heisman Trophy as the nation's top player, Chase won the Fred Biletnikoff Award, which is given to the nation's best receiver.

Breaking records was nothing new to Chase, who had done the same thing at Archbishop Rummel High in Metairie, Louisiana. Rummel head coach Jay Roth had employed a run-heavy, I-formation offense for the more than two decades he had helmed the Raiders. But during one game in 2016, he watched Ja'Marr, then a junior, catch four balls for 226 yards and four touchdowns. Roth decided then and there he needed to implement a new offense to make full use of Ja'Marr's receiving talents.

So Roth studied several pass-happy offenses and incorporated them into Ja'Marr's senior season. The standout ended the year with 1,011 yards and 15 touchdowns on 61 receptions, which were more catches than most Rummel players on the school's all-time receiving list had totaled in their entire careers.

Many universities battled to secure a commitment from the five-star phenom, but LSU head coach Ed Orgeron was not about to let the most talented player in the state leave home. To demonstrate Chase's importance to the Tiger football program, the entire coaching staff—even the defensive ones—showed up at the Chase household a week before signing day to beg for his services. The gambit paid off.

Before the Bengals paired Burrow with Chase in 2021, the franchise hadn't won a play-off game since January 6, 1991, and it hadn't played in a Super Bowl since the 1988 season. In year one of the Chase-Burrow era, the Bengals ended both droughts, surprising everyone by winning at Kansas City for the right to play—and eventually lose to—the Los Angeles Rams in Super Bowl LVI. Chase was named Offensive Rookie of the Year and made the Pro Bowl, backing his inaugural season with a second Pro Bowl in year two.

Whether in high school, college, or the pros, Chase has proven to be a winner.

Position: **Wide Receiver**
Hometown: **Harvey, LA**
Born: **Mar. 1, 2000**
Height: **6'1"**
Weight: **200 lb.**
Team: **Cincinnati Bengals**
Career Yards per Reception: **14.9**

Trevon Diggs

Dallas Cowboys cornerback Trevon Diggs has two secret weapons. First, he played wide receiver through his freshman year at the University of Alabama, and so he has an intimate understanding of route running. So he may very well know which route a receiver is running before the receiver even executes it.

Trevon's second secret weapon, however, is his most powerful one: his older brother Stefon Diggs. Stefon, five years older than Trevon, is a star wide receiver for the Buffalo Bills. A three-time Pro Bowler who led the league in receptions and yards in 2020, Stefon is considered one of the best receivers in the game. And that is the player Trevon competed against day in, day out as a kid. Perhaps that's why Trevon is very rarely impressed with any receiver he's up against. Battling his brother as they grew up in Gaithersburg, Maryland, helped prepare Trevon for anything an NFL offense could throw at him.

But Stefon is much more than a training partner and brother—Stefon is a father figure to his little brother. In January 2008, when Trevon was nine and Stefon was 14, their father Aron died of congestive heart failure. Prior to his passing, Aron had given Stefon a mission: to take care of Trevon. It was a directive Stefon took to heart. Although he was one of the top players in his class, Stefon signed with the University of Maryland so he could stay close to his brother.

Before his health failed him, it had been Aron who had taken the reins from a football standpoint. He had signed Trevon up to play football when Trevon turned five and would quiz Trevon on formations as they watched NFL games. Aron would also take the boys to run bleachers and sprints after school. After Aron passed, Stefon stepped into their father's role, dragging Trevon to workouts each day.

Having a superstar older brother does have drawbacks. Trevon played high school ball at the Avalon School in Wheaton, Maryland. There, he felt his peers thought he hadn't earned his reputation as a top player, but was just riding Stefon's coattails. So when the time came to choose a college, he decided to forge his own path and go to Alabama instead.

Diggs began his collegiate career at wide receiver and safety, but coach Nick Saban moved him to cornerback after his freshman year. It was not a smooth transition, and Diggs lost his starting spot as a sophomore. He then broke his foot six games into his junior year. Stefon encouraged him to keep working, and Diggs had an outstanding senior year, with three interceptions and two defensive touchdowns. For his efforts, he earned third-team All American status.

The Cowboys selected Diggs in the second round of the 2020 NFL draft. His breakout year came in 2021, when he tied an NFL record with seven interceptions in the first six games of the season. He ended up leading the league with 11 interceptions that year—the most by any NFL player in 40 years. Trevon Diggs was a first-team All-Pro that year and has made the Pro Bowl in each of the last two seasons.

Nobody accuses Trevon as simply riding Stefon's coattails anymore.

Position: **Cornerback**
Hometown: **Gaithersburg, MD**
Born: **Sept. 20, 1998**
Height: **6'2"**
Weight: **195 lb.**
Team: **Dallas Cowboys**
Career Interceptions: **17**

Aaron Donald

Los Angeles Rams defensive tackle Aaron Donald had a dream that stretched back to his boyhood days in Pittsburgh. Back then, Aaron shared a room with his older brother Archie Jr., and they would often fantasize about one day making enough money to help their parents retire. So when Aaron signed a six-year, $135 million contract prior to the 2018 season, the first thing he did was call his parents. When his father Archie answered the phone, Aaron told him the time had come to retire; he would be taking care of them. A son's lifelong dream had become a reality.

Archie Donald had grown up without a father. He vowed things would be different with him, and he was a loving presence in his children's lives. In his youth, Archie had once won a weightlifting competition by benching 405 pounds. Years later, as his son Aaron was making a name for himself on the football field, Archie worried about Aaron's work ethic—or lack thereof. So when Aaron was a freshman at Penn Hills High School, Archie invited his youngest son to work out with him in the homemade gymnasium he had in the basement of the house. Wake-up time was 4:30 a.m.

Aaron was reluctant at first, but when he noticed the positive changes the workouts were having on his body, he fully bought into the program.

The average NFL defensive tackle is 6'3" and 310 pounds. Aaron Donald topped out at 6'1" and only weighs 280 pounds. So even after a distinguished high school career, not many schools were interested in the undersized Donald. One coach who was, however, was University of Pittsburgh's Dave Wannstedt, who persuaded Donald to play for him. The plan was to have Donald redshirt his freshman year, but after just a few practices, defensive line coach Greg Romeus approached Wannstedt and asked him to reconsider. Donald was making too many plays to sit.

By his senior year, Donald was an All-American. Still, concerns about his size persisted. One person who wasn't hung up on his size was then St. Louis Rams defensive line coach Mike Waufle, who considered Donald the best college player he'd ever seen. He pushed hard for the Rams to draft him. And the team listened, taking Donald with the 13th pick of the 2014 NFL draft.

Waufle's instinct proved prescient. Donald made the Pro Bowl his rookie year and hasn't missed one yet in his nine-year career. In 2018, he set the record for most sacks by a defensive tackle, getting to the quarterback 20.5 times. He is one of three players—JJ Watt and Lawrence Taylor being the others—in NFL history named Defensive Player of the Year three times. He's been a first-team All-Pro seven times and helped the Rams win Super Bowl LVI after the 2021 season.

On top of all that, Donald has found time to go back to Pittsburgh and finish his degree, and he established the AD99 Solutions Foundation in Pittsburgh that reaches out to underprivileged kids through athletics and community-based projects. And sometimes, in the off-season, he still returns to that basement weight room—dubbed "The Dungeon"—to work out with his dad, the man who inspired Aaron's dreams and helped make them come true.

Position: **Defensive Tackle**
Hometown: **Pittsburgh, PA**
Born: **May 23, 1991**
Height: **6'1"**
Weight: **280 lb.**
Team: **Los Angeles Rams**
Career Sacks: **103**

Sauce Gardner

Detroit-based youth football coach Curtez Harris, known throughout the city as Coach Tez, had a habit of giving all of his players nicknames. After one game, Coach Tez was complimenting one of his players on a nasty cutback move—a six-year-old named Ahmad Gardner—when he all of the sudden blurted out, "A1 Sauce Sweet Feet Gardner." The exuberant Gardner fell in love with the name, eventually shortening it to Sauce. Now entering just his second year with the New York Jets, Sauce Gardner is already one of the most feared cornerbacks in the league.

These days, Sauce is more than just a name: it's an alter ego. While Ahmad is soft-spoken, thoughtful, and calm, Sauce is brimming with bravado and confidence. Week after week, year after year, it is Sauce that shows up on game day. In three years at the University of Cincinnati, Gardner didn't give up a single touchdown. That led him to become the fourth overall player taken in the 2022 NFL draft. And Gardner's strong play continued. He was named Defensive Rookie of the Year, and was a first-team All-Pro and a Pro Bowler after giving up just 54 yards total in man coverage all season.

Sauce Gardner's rise was far from inevitable. The youngest of three children, Ahmad grew up on Detroit's Near East Side, a tough area known for its fair share of violence. He credits his mom Alisa for keeping him on the straight and narrow. Alisa would constantly encourage him to stand out from his peers and take a different route from the one they so often were on. To this day, Gardner says he has never drank or smoked. Although money was tight, Alisa also always found a way to pay for Sauce's various football camps, which were important opportunities for the talented player to gain exposure. No wonder Gardner considers Alisa his superhero.

Playing at Martin Luther King High School, Sauce wasn't as heavily recruited as his talent might suggest. This was in part because of his size: He was barely 160 pounds at the time. Up until his junior year, he also primarily played wide receiver. Then in one game, an emergency need opened up in the secondary when two of Sauce's teammates collided and injured themselves. Sauce stepped in and dazzled, and he became a permanent fixture at cornerback. It was then that the college offers started piling up.

Still, his slight stature scared away some of the bigger brands, including Michigan and Michigan State right in Gardner's backyard. So he ended up signing with Cincinnati, with head coach Luke Fickell envisioning Gardner as more of a developmental prospect. But Gardner kept standing out in practice, and when he got a chance to see the field against nationally ranked University of Central Florida, his pick-six helped the Bearcats pull off the upset. That was the nation's first glimpse of Sauce Gardner's dominance. It wouldn't be the last.

Position: **Cornerback**
Hometown: **Detroit, MI**
Born: **Aug. 31, 2000**
Height: **6'3"**
Weight: **200 lb.**
Team: **New York Jets**
Career Interceptions: **2**

Myles Garrett

Cleveland Browns All-Pro defensive end Myles Garrett was practically destined for athletic greatness. His mother Audrey was an All-American at the 60-meter hurdles at Hampton in the early 1980s. His older sister Brea won the 2014 NCAA indoor championship in the weight throw as a junior at Texas A&M. And his brother Sean Williams, nearly a decade older than Myles, was the 17th pick of the 2007 NBA draft out of Boston College.

Garrett no doubt possesses the genes necessary to reach the highest echelons of the sporting world, and the 6'4", 272-pound Texan was a physical wonder from an early age.

As a 16-year-old, while Sean was playing for the NBA's Dallas Mavericks, Myles would often play his brother one-on-one at the team's facility. Mavericks general manager Donnie Nelson called Sean's agent one day and told him these intense games had to stop out of fear Sean would get hurt. Nelson didn't know who Myles was, but he assumed the teenager was one of Sean's bodyguards.

It is little wonder, then, that Myles was ranked as the No. 2 overall football recruit in the U.S. when he was at Arlington (Texas) Martin High School. Just about every college program in the country wanted him. Texas A&M had a unique advantage, though, as Brea would stop by the football office to give the coaches advice on how best to woo her brother.

And while the family connection eventually won out, another one of Garrett's passions nearly took him down a different path. Growing up in Arlington, Myles had a fascination with dinosaurs, and specifically Jurassic Park. He would dig for fossils in his backyard, bringing small rocks to his father and claiming they were dinosaur teeth. That love affair has never truly gone extinct, and he seriously considered enrolling at Ohio State because of the university's renowned paleontology program. At Texas A&M, Garrett minored in geology and still plans on pursuing paleontology in the future.

As for the present, the first pick of the 2017 NFL draft will continue terrorizing NFL quarterbacks with his combination of size, strength, speed, and skill. In his first six seasons as a professional, Garrett has already made four Pro Bowls and been named a first-team All-Pro twice. In 2022, he tied his career high with 16 sacks, and he has recorded double-digit sacks in every year since he finished with seven sacks in his injury-plagued rookie season.

Position: **Defensive End**
Hometown: **Arlington, TX**
Born: **Dec. 29, 1995**
Height: **6'4"**
Weight: **272 lb.**
Team: **Cleveland Browns**
Career Sacks: **74.5**

Derrick Henry

Gladys Henry experienced a feeling of shock when she first laid eyes on her grandson Derrick. His birth had come as a surprise to the entire family because of how young Derrick's parents were at the time. His mother was 15 and his father 16. So Gladys gave the baby his first nickname: Shocka.

It has become quite the appropriate moniker. The Tennessee Titans running back has been shocking people with his on-field exploits for most of his life, first during his prep days at Yulee High School in Florida. All he did there was set the national high school career rushing record by amassing 12,123 yards over his four seasons.

From there, he attended the University of Alabama. In 2015, as a junior, Henry set the Southeastern Conference single-season record by rushing for 2,219 yards. That year, he won the Doak Walker Award, which is given to the best running back in the nation, and the Heisman Trophy, which is awarded to the best overall college football player.

NFL defenses have had about as much luck stopping the 6'3", 247-pound Henry as high school and college ones did. Since the Titans selected Henry with the 45th overall pick of the 2016 draft, Henry has established himself as one of the most imposing and intimidating backs in the league. In 2018, he tied an NFL record when he rushed for a 99-yard touchdown against Jacksonville. He led the entire league in rushing the next two years, including becoming just the eighth player in history to exceed 2,000 yards in 2020. All of these accomplishments have earned Shocka a new nickname: King Henry.

Though he may be the king now, Henry comes from rather humble beginnings. Because of his parents' youth—and his father's frequent run-ins with the law—Gladys agreed to raise Derrick. She had had some experience raising children, as she had 14 of her own. Derrick learned the meaning of hard work from Gladys, who would leave early each morning to clean rooms at the Holiday Inn only to cook and clean for Derrick each evening when she got home.

Gladys passed away in 2016, but her influence on Henry persists to this day. Henry promised Gladys he would get his college degree. After all, she would remind him, football wouldn't last forever. So even though he left Alabama after his junior year, Henry went back to school and earned that degree in 2018. After all she did for him, there was no way Shocka was going to break that promise.

Position: **Running Back**
Hometown: **Yulee, FL**
Born: **Jan. 4, 1994**
Height: **6'3"**
Weight: **247 lb.**
Team: **Tennessee Titans**
Career Rushing Touchdowns: **78**

Jalen Hurts

Philadelphia Eagles fourth-year quarterback Jalen Hurts, coming off the sting of losing the most recent Super Bowl to rival QB Patrick Mahomes of the Kansas City Chiefs, is no stranger to adversity—not after what he experienced in his college career.

A conflicted and distraught Hurts sat in a hotel room with his family the night the University of Alabama won the 2017 National Championship, tears streaming down his face. It should have been the most triumphant moment in the sophomore's life, but the game hadn't unfolded as planned. With Hurts struggling and the Crimson Tide down 13–0 at halftime against the Georgia Bulldogs, legendary coach Nick Saban had benched Hurts in favor of backup Tua Tagovailoa, who led an epic comeback.

Up to that point, all Hurts had done in his first two seasons was put together a 26–2 record as a starter while guiding Alabama to back-to-back National Championship games. But despite that, his place on the team was now uncertain. "What are we going to do now?" Jalen asked his father Averion. "We are going to fight," the elder Hurts replied.

Jalen Hurts has long demonstrated a maturity beyond his years. He enrolled early at Alabama, arriving on campus following the 2015 regular season as a 17-year-old. He was thrown into the fire immediately, tasked with helping Alabama's defense prepare for that season's National Championship game by running the scout team offense. He impressed the veterans and the coaching staff with his poise while displaying almost endless potential. Then, prior to the second game of the 2016 season, Saban

named Hurts the starter. It would be the first time since 1984 that a freshman quarterback started a game for Alabama.

Hurts attributes much of his success to his father, a high school football coach in Channelview, Texas. Being a coach's son afforded Jalen an opportunity to witness his father handling conflicts and adversity, inspiring people, and building relationships. By watching his father, Jalen learned how to lead.

And leaders don't jump ship when the going gets tough. So, Hurts stuck with Alabama during the 2018 season, playing a reserve role that year. But in a delicious bit of irony, Hurts came in for an injured Tagovailoa during the SEC Championship and led Alabama to a come-from-behind victory—on the same field where he had been benched.

Following the 2018 season, Hurts decided to finish his college football career at the University of Oklahoma, where he led the Sooners to a Big 12 Championship and an appearance in the College Football Playoff. That means Hurts's teams made the playoffs in each year of his college career. He also finished second in the Heisman Trophy voting.

Winning has followed Hurts to the NFL. The Eagles selected Hurts in the second round of the 2020 NFL draft, and he took over as the starter late into his rookie campaign. He had a breakthrough year in 2022, making his first Pro Bowl and finishing second to Mahomes in the MVP race. Hurts also led Philadelphia to an NFC Championship. And despite the Super Bowl loss, Philadelphia has a bright future. After all, their quarterback is quite the fighter.

Position: **Quarterback**
Hometown: **Houston, TX**
Born: **Aug. 7, 1998**
Height: **6'1"**
Weight: **223 lb.**
Team: **Philadelphia Eagles**
Career QB Rating: **92.2**

Josh Jacobs

When running back Josh Jacobs signed his first NFL contract after being selected in the first round by the Raiders in 2019, he earned a $6.7 million signing bonus. And he knew exactly what he wanted to do with it: Buy his father a house. After all, for a large portion of his childhood, he and his family didn't have one.

When Josh was in the fourth grade growing up in Tulsa, Oklahoma, his parents split up. His father Marty eventually won custody of all five of his children. Already struggling to make ends meet, Marty lost his job shortly thereafter. Unable to pay the rent, Marty lost his apartment. For the next couple of years, the Jacobs family would bounce from motel to motel, sometimes even spending nights sleeping in their car.

Marty also had trouble feeding his five children. Their diet consisted of a lot of white rice and ramen noodles. On good days, their motel would have a continental breakfast, and they would grab enough food for the entire day. On bad days, there wasn't enough food to go around. On those days, Marty wouldn't eat.

Even so, Marty always stayed upbeat and optimistic. He would encourage his children to express themselves, whether it was through freestyle rapping, writing poetry, or drawing. Jacobs remembers spending nights laughing together as a family. A man of deep faith, Marty believed that if he continued to work hard, persevere, and live life the right way, things would work out. He reminded his children that the easy way out usually isn't the right way.

Finally, when Josh was in the eighth grade, Marty found stable work. Though money was still tight, at least they had a home. Little did they realize that, thanks to Josh's talents, their lives were about to be transformed.

Josh put up monster numbers as a running back at McLain High School. Unfortunately, the school was not known for producing quality football players, and so Josh's feats went largely unnoticed. It wasn't until December of his senior year that he garnered his first scholarship offer from a big-time college football program.

Then, a man named Gerald Smith, who helps high school players get recruited, stumbled on Josh's tape. He reached out and told Josh to start a Twitter account and post his highlights. Whatever Smith did worked, because within days Josh was getting bombarded with offers.

He ended up choosing to play at the University of Alabama. Even so, Jacobs didn't have the NFL in mind. He was just excited to be the first person in his family to go to college. But after an outstanding junior season, he was considered the top running back prospect in the 2019 NFL draft, and all his hard work paid off when the Raiders called his name with the 24th overall pick.

In his first year, Jacobs broke the Raiders' rookie rushing record of Hall of Famer Marcus Allen as the first rookie in franchise history to break 1,000 yards. He made the Pro Bowl in his second year, and in 2022 he led the league in rushing with 1,653 yards. He earned first-team All-Pro status in the process. More importantly, he has ensured his family will never have to worry about money ever again.

Position: **Running Back**
Hometown: **Tulsa, OK**
Born: **Feb. 11, 1998**
Height: **5'10"**
Weight: **220 lb.**
Team: **Las Vegas Raiders**
Career Rushing TDs: **40**

Derwin James Jr.

Los Angeles Chargers safety Derwin James Jr. takes after his father. The elder James is still a legend down in Haines City, Florida, for the ferociousness with which he played the game of football. Back then, they called him Blue because his hits left marks that turned that color. Unfortunately, poor grades and a knee injury prevented James Sr. from capitalizing on his sizable athletic talents. Fortunately, though, he was able to pass those traits on to his son.

Derwin Sr. and Shanita Williams knew early on they had something special with their firstborn son. His first word, after all, was "ball." At the age of four, Derwin Jr. was able to join the youth football team his father coached after some relentless begging. The other kids on the team were all six and seven.

The coach of Auburndale (Florida) High School had a simple, hard-and-fast rule: no freshman on the varsity team—ever. And he stuck to that until Derwin James Jr. came on the scene. The defensive coaches—who had already identified Derwin as a unique talent—almost in unison told the coach he had to put Derwin on the field. He was already one of the best players on the squad.

How good was he? When longtime Florida State University assistant coach Odell Haggins first saw Derwin play, he couldn't believe the talented kid was just a freshman. He decided to play a joke on FSU head coach Jimbo Fisher by showing him James's film and telling him the boy was a senior. Fisher berated Haggins for not identifying James as a potential recruit earlier. When told the truth, Fisher said they had to offer the kid a scholarship—immediately. A couple of days later, Haggins did just that, and the freshman committed to the Seminoles on the spot.

At FSU, James made his presence felt right away, earning Freshman All-American honors from various outlets in 2015. A knee injury forced him to miss much of his sophomore season, but he came back with a vengeance as a junior and was named a first-team All-American by the Football Writers Association of America. He declared for the NFL draft afterward, and the Chargers selected him with the 17th pick.

Unsurprisingly, he was named a first-team All-Pro after his rookie year, and he has made the Pro Bowl in every year he has remained healthy. This past off-season, the Chargers showed their faith in James by signing him to a four-year contract extension that makes him the league's highest-paid safety. Some highly ranked athletes fail to live up to the hype. Others, like Derwin James Jr., exceed it.

Position: **Strong Safety**
Hometown: **Haines City, FL**
Born: **Aug. 3, 1996**
Height: **6'2"**
Weight: **215 lb.**
Team: **Los Angeles Chargers**
Career Interceptions: **7**

Justin Jefferson

Minnesota Vikings wide receiver Justin Jefferson has had an explosive start to his NFL career. The 22nd pick of the 2020 draft set the record for most receiving yards by a rookie in the Super Bowl era (since 1966) by compiling 1,400 yards on 88 receptions—and that after he didn't even start the first two games. He followed that up with a 1,616-yard season in 2021 before leading the league in yards (1,809) and receptions (128) this past season, earning his third-straight Pro Bowl designation while being named a first-team All-Pro.

And yet, it wasn't so long ago that Justin Jefferson was struggling to garner any attention on the gridiron. The youngest son of John and Elaine Jefferson always had some big shoes to fill. His oldest brother Jordan played quarterback at Louisiana State University from 2008 until 2011, when the Tigers fell one win short of a national championship. His other brother Rickey played safety for LSU from 2013 to 2016.

From a young age, Justin wanted to be just like his brothers. Sometimes, when Jordan and Rickey were playing video games, they would give Justin a controller to let him feel like he was playing as well. As a three-year-old, he would sit on the bench of Rickey's little league basketball games, convinced he was part of the team.

But for a while, it looked like Justin wouldn't quite live up to his brothers' legacies. He entered Destrehan High School in Louisiana at a slight 5'7" and 125 pounds. While Rickey had played varsity as a freshman, Justin was relegated to the freshman team. By his senior year, Justin had sprouted to 6'2" and put up solid numbers. Still, he was ranked just the 308th-best receiver in the class of 2017, and his only offers came from Tulane, Nicholls State, Northwestern—and LSU.

While poor grades kept most big-time schools away, Tigers head coach Ed Orgeron, who had forged a close relationship with the Jeffersons, told Justin a scholarship was waiting for him as soon as he was ready. Justin buckled down his senior year, and that summer he even took a summer class in order to graduate. Finally, he was ready. In August, he at last followed in his brothers' footsteps and joined the LSU Tigers as their final scholarship member.

After receiving scant playing time as a freshman, Jefferson had a solid sophomore season in 2018 before truly breaking out in 2019. On a loaded team that included Heisman Trophy–winning quarterback Joe Burrow and All-American receiver Ja'Marr Chase, Jefferson caught 111 balls for 1,540 yards and 18 touchdowns, including four touchdowns in the first half of the College Football Playoff semifinal game against Oklahoma. Justin would one-up his brother Jordan that year by bringing home a national championship for LSU.

Afterward, Jefferson declared for the NFL draft, and he's been tearing up the league ever since. No, Justin hasn't lived up to his brothers' legacies—he's far surpassed them.

Position: **Wide Receiver**
Hometown: **St. Rose, LA**
Born: **June 16, 1999**
Height: **6'1"**
Weight: **195 lb.**
Team: **Minnesota Vikings**
Career Receptions: **324**

Jason Kelce

Most people who stand 6 feet, 3 inches tall and weigh 295 pounds never get described as "undersized." Philadelphia Eagles center Jason Kelce, however, has had that descriptor dog him his entire football career. If nothing else, then, his five first-team All-Pro honors, six Pro Bowls, two Super Bowl appearances, and one championship have proven once and for all that size isn't everything.

Growing up in Cleveland Heights, Ohio, Jason and his younger brother Travis—himself a future Hall of Fame tight end for the Kansas City Chiefs—pushed each other toward greatness. Travis was constantly battling for Jason's respect; Jason was never inclined to take it easy on his younger sibling. The result, according to their mother Donna, was a lot of fighting—and sometimes the need for home repairs. For instance, Travis once bet that Jason couldn't throw a football over their three-story house, which led to a broken window and a trip to the hardware store.

That same competitiveness also translated into success in sports. For Jason, that meant excelling at hockey, baseball, and, of course, football. In high school, Jason did a little bit of everything for Cleveland Heights: running back, long snapper, middle linebacker. In his senior year as team captain, he won the league's defensive MVP award. But at "only" 225 pounds at the time, no Division I team offered him a scholarship, and he considered playing at the Division II level.

Instead, he decided to bet on himself and walked on to the University of Cincinnati's football team. A coaching change after a freshman year spent on the scout team altered Kelce's destiny. New coach Brian Kelly was installing a new offense that required more athletic offensive linemen. He approached Kelce about a position change. Kelce, never one to let an opportunity slip by, agreed on one condition: He wanted a scholarship. Coach Kelly granted the brazen request, and Kelce got to work, both on learning a new position and putting on weight.

The switch fit Kelce well. His experience at linebacker helped him read defensive schemes. Coach Kelly's system utilized Kelce's speed and athleticism and minimized any reliance on brute strength and power. With Kelce's help, Cincinnati recorded its first three double-digit-win seasons in school history.

With his college eligibility up following the 2010 season, Kelce once again had to face questions surrounding his size. Even though he ran the fastest 40-yard dash of any lineman in his class at 4.89 seconds, he had to wait until the sixth round of the 2011 NFL draft. The Eagles, coached then by offensive guru Andy Reid, selected Jason with the 191st pick.

Now in his 13th year, it is safe to say a lot of people at many levels underestimated Jason Kelce. He's only the third center since 1970 to be named a first-team All-Pro five times. The other two are in the Hall of Fame. He helped bring the Eagles a Super Bowl win in 2018. Last season, the Eagles made the Super Bowl again, falling to Travis's Chiefs. It was the first time brothers squared off in a Super Bowl. In other words, there has been nothing "undersized" about Jason's career.

Position: **Center**
Hometown: **Cleveland Heights, OH**
Born: **Nov. 5, 1987**
Height: **6'3"**
Weight: **295 lb.**
Team: **Philadelphia Eagles**
Fact: **Five-Time First-Team All-Pro**

Travis Kelce

Kansas City Chiefs tight end Travis Kelce and his older brother, Philadelphia Eagles center Jason Kelce, got into countless fights growing up in Cleveland Heights, Ohio. Constantly competing against one another, neither boy could deal with losing at anything–basketball, hockey, lacrosse, etc.–at the hands of the other. But when Travis needed Jason the most, his big brother came through. Travis's entire career depended on it.

Both brothers demonstrated athletic talent early on, racking up trophies in a variety of sports. Aside from football, Travis played basketball while Jason played hockey. They both played baseball. Travis developed into the more sought-after athlete. While Jason received no scholarship offers out of high school and ended up walking on to the University of Cincinnati's football team, Travis, who was his high school's star quarterback, had many options. Ultimately, he chose to follow his brother as a Bearcat.

But just as Jason's career was beginning to blossom after he moved from linebacker to the offensive line, Travis's was bottoming out. At the end of his redshirt freshman year, Travis failed a drug test. When new head coach Butch Jones arrived the following year, he dismissed Travis from the team in a move meant to overhaul the team's culture. Travis's housing was also revoked, forcing him to move in with Jason and get a job administering phone surveys.

Later that season, though, Jason walked into a coaches' meeting and stuck his neck out for his little brother. He told them that he had earned the right to be listened to and they had to trust him that letting Travis back on the team was the right decision. Jason's experience must have carried some weight because Travis Kelce rejoined the squad for his junior season.

To say the younger Kelce has made the most of his second chance is the ultimate understatement. He even made the dean's list that first fall back with the team (an accomplishment Travis's father Ed said "was unheard of"). The 6'5", 256-pound athletic machine then broke out during his senior year, catching 45 passes for 722 yards and eight touchdowns. The Chiefs selected him in the third round of the 2013 draft. Since then, Kelce has been on the fast track to the Hall of Fame.

No tight end in the history of the NFL has had as many 1,000-yard seasons as Kelce, who has done it for seven consecutive years and counting. He holds the single-season record for tight ends in receiving yards, at 1,416, and his career average of 71.8 yards per game is also first all-time for his position. He's made the last eight Pro Bowls and is a four-time first-team All-Pro selection. Along the way, he's also helped the Chiefs win two Super Bowls, including last season's victory over Jason's Eagles! (Jason, a six-time Pro Bowler and onetime Super Bowl champ, has done all right for himself, too.)

But none of Travis Kelce's many accomplishments could have happened if not for an assist from his big brother.

Position: **Tight End**
Hometown: **Cleveland Heights, OH**
Born: **Oct. 5, 1989**
Height: **6'5"**
Weight: **256 lb.**
Team: **Kansas City Chiefs**
Career Receiving Yards: **10,344**

George Kittle

It was a long pause for such a simple question. San Francisco tight end George Kittle had been asked by a reporter if he has ever had a bad day. Fourteen seconds of pondering later, Kittle looked up and said no. It may seem improbable—impossible even—for that to be the case. Surely Kittle isn't being entirely honest with himself.

Then again, those closest to the player also struggle to remember the All-Pro ever having a bad day. His father Bruce certainly can't. Neither can his mother Jan Krieger. What about his wife Claire? Not to her recollection. Kittle's college coach Kirk Ferentz of the University of Iowa and former high school coach Greg Nation also answer in the negative. Maybe, then, just maybe Kittle is being truthful. After all, he is having too much fun playing football to have a bad day.

The 6'4", 250-pound Kittle was destined to play football. Bruce Kittle had been on the offensive line at Iowa, captaining the 1981 team that won the Big Ten Championship and played in the Rose Bowl. Jan Krieger was no slouch of an athlete herself. The Iowa high school Hall of Famer played basketball and softball at Drake.

George Kittle was even born on a college football Saturday. His parents were living in Madison, Wisconsin, at the time, and Bruce, with the eventual help of a police escort, had to fight through game-day traffic—the Badgers were taking on Northwestern that day—to make it to the hospital. His parents made sure George's football accompanied him in his crib each night.

The future star's larger-than-life personality revealed itself early. Attending a Wisconsin game as a four-year-old, George ran down 15 rows to the front when the band started playing and began to dance. Fans were so entertained, they began throwing quarters at him. Bruce reckons his son made about five dollars that day.

Fun was a word used frequently in the Kittle home. In fact, the last words Bruce still tells George before each game are, "Go have fun." The sentiment goes back at least one more generation. George's grandma's favorite expression is, "You have to take your good times with ya." Kittle has never forgotten what it feels like to be a little kid enjoying the game as a fan.

Kittle's rise to NFL stardom came seemingly out of nowhere. Iowa offered him its final available scholarship out of high school only after two other recruits turned the Hawkeyes down. In his entire four-year tenure at Iowa, Kittle caught just 48 passes for 737 yards. That lack of production, though partly the result of a run-first offense and several injuries, caused Kittle to fall to the fifth round of the 2017 NFL draft when San Francisco selected him with the 146th overall pick.

Kittle burst onto the scene in his second season in 2018. That year, he set the single-season record for most receiving yards by a TE, at 1,377 yards (a record since broken by Kansas City's Travis Kelce). He followed that up with 1,053 receiving yards in 2019, and he has made the Pro Bowl four times in the last five years. With a career like Kittle's, it's easier to fathom him never having a bad day.

Position: **Tight End**
Hometown: **Madison, WI**
Born: **Oct. 9, 1993**
Height: **6'4"**
Weight: **250 lb.**
Team: **San Francisco 49ers**
Career Receptions: **395**

Dexter Lawrence

Dexter Lawrence entered the world on the lighter side at only 6 pounds, 9 ounces, but the New York Giants defensive lineman quickly made up ground—and then some. By the fifth grade he was already 5'11" and 270 pounds. Now, the Pro Bowler out of Clemson checks in at 6'4" and a svelte 342 pounds, making him a nightmare for opposing offenses to block.

Dexter started playing football in fifth grade, but he nearly gave up the game when he got to Wake Forest (North Carolina) High School. Dexter wanted to focus on basketball, and he had no interest in playing on the school's junior varsity football team. As it turns out, football coach Reggie Lucas also had no interest in putting Dexter with the junior varsity. Recognizing the generational talent he had on his hands, Lucas invited Dexter to play varsity. The teenager accepted and became a starter—one of the first freshmen in the school's history to do so. On his very first play of his very first high school game, Dexter tackled the ball carrier for a loss. A star was born.

By the time Dexter was a senior, multiple scouting services had him ranked the No. 2 overall football recruit in the nation. It wasn't just his size that set him apart, but how he was able to move at that size. His unnatural athleticism really came through on the basketball court, where he proved to be quite light-footed. He could even propel his massive frame high enough in the air to dunk. To those who knew Dexter's family, none of this was all too surprising. His mother Julia Parker had run track at the University of Arkansas at Pine Bluff. His father Dexter Lawrence Sr. had been a linebacker at Arkansas State. His younger brother Devon would play running back for North Carolina.

As for Dexter, he had his pick of any school in the country. Clemson eventually won the Lawrence sweepstakes—and not merely because of its football powerhouse status, though that probably didn't hurt. Lawrence had always taken his studies seriously, attending math camps in his youth and graduating high school a semester early. He wanted to go somewhere with strong academics, and at Clemson he pursued a degree in justice studies, with a goal of entering the field of forensics.

But Lawrence's crime-solving aspirations will have to wait for now. He first dominated at Clemson like he did in high school, helping the Tigers win two national championships in his three-year college career. He then left school a year early, and the Giants selected him with the 17th pick of the 2019 draft. Though solid through his first three seasons, Dexter didn't really break out until year four. In 2022, the Giants tweaked where Lawrence lined up, putting him directly over the center instead of up over larger guards. The move worked, and Lawrence set career highs in both tackles and sacks while earning his first trip to the Pro Bowl and leading New York to a surprise playoff berth.

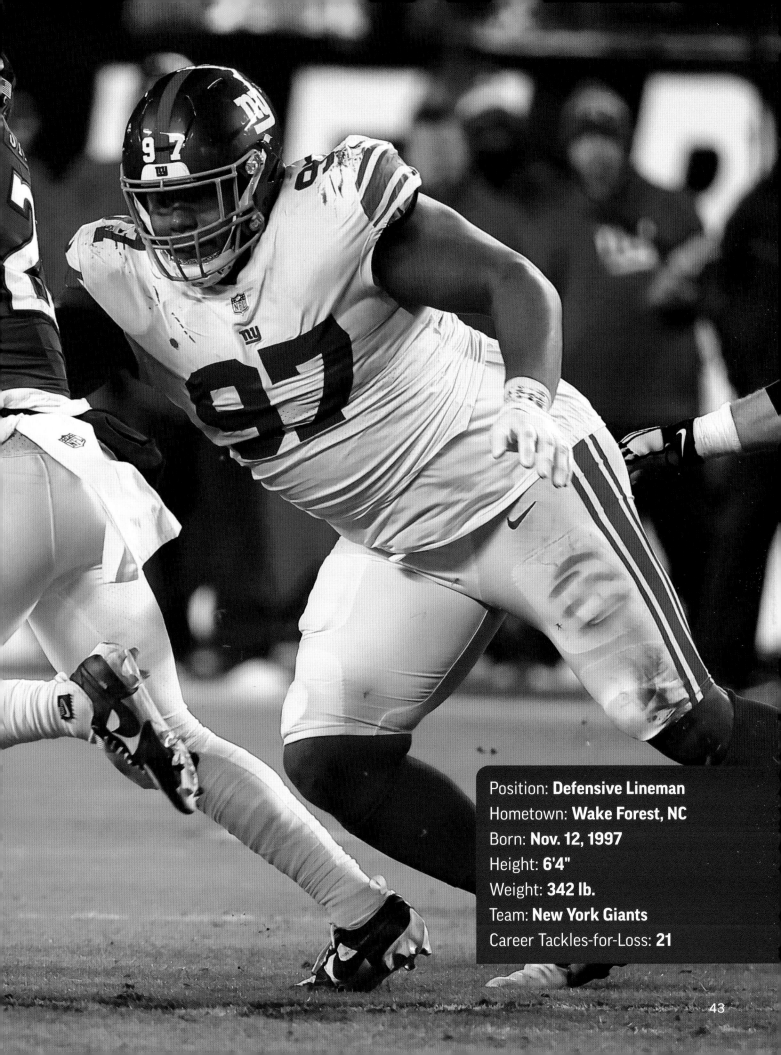

Position: **Defensive Lineman**
Hometown: **Wake Forest, NC**
Born: **Nov. 12, 1997**
Height: **6'4"**
Weight: **342 lb.**
Team: **New York Giants**
Career Tackles-for-Loss: **21**

Patrick Mahomes

The Kansas City Chiefs already had a good quarterback. In 2016, Alex Smith had led them to their first AFC West divisional championship since 2010, making the Pro Bowl in the process. So it was surprising when the team traded up 17 slots in the 2017 draft to select a quarterback in the first round. People may have questioned that decision back then, but nobody does now. That's because the player the Chiefs drafted–Patrick Mahomes–has set a new standard for the QB position.

Patrick Mahomes learned what it takes to excel at professional sports at a very young age. His father Pat pitched for six Major League Baseball teams over a 12-year period, and his young son was a constant presence along the way. Patrick shagged fly balls during batting practice, met Derek Jeter, took turns hitting balls off of a tee with Alex Rodriguez, and was on the field during a World Series. He saw firsthand the amount of work these great athletes put into their craft day in and day out.

While Patrick may have been destined to be an athlete, his father never wanted him to play football. As a kid, Patrick was drawn more to baseball and basketball, and his father hoped his son would go down one of those roads. Patrick was on Whitehouse High School's football team as a sophomore, playing safety. Going into his junior season, though, he nearly quit because he didn't think the coaches were giving him a fair shot to try at quarterback. Patrick decided to stick it out, and his prayers were answered when he was named the starting quarterback. He's never looked back. As a senior, he threw for 4,619 yards and 50 touchdowns and committed to play college ball at Texas Tech.

He started his Red Raiders career as the backup, but got his chance when starter Davis Webb got injured. After a slow start, Mahomes began to catch fire, averaging 464 yards his last two games, including setting a conference freshman record by throwing for 598 yards against Baylor. The next year, Mahomes won the starting job and continued to post eye-popping numbers. Still, there were questions surrounding Mahomes heading into the 2017 draft, in part because of the "Air Raid" offense Texas Tech employed. Air Raid quarterbacks had a tendency to put up big numbers that didn't translate into NFL success. That is because the offense doesn't require a strong arm and most of the play-calling is done by the coach.

The Chiefs, though, had done their homework. Before the draft, head coach Andy Reid created a mock "install" day to teach Mahomes part of their offense. After a break, Reid tested the player's retention by having him turn around and install the offense to Reid. Mahomes did so effortlessly. When the draft arrived, the Chiefs were determined to get their man.

Mahomes was afforded the luxury of sitting out and learning from Smith during his rookie season before starting in 2018. Since then, the Chiefs have never won fewer than 12 games and have reached three Super Bowls, winning twice. Mahomes has made the Pro Bowl every year since 2018 and has been a first-team All-Pro twice. From the time he became the full-time starter, no quarterback has thrown for more yards than Mahomes (23,957) or TDs (192). With all due respect to Smith, the Chiefs' decision to pivot to Mahomes was nothing short of a grand slam home run.

Position: **Quarterback**
Hometown: **Tyler, TX**
Born: **Sept. 17, 1995**
Height: **6'2"**
Weight: **225 lb.**
Team: **Kansas City Chiefs**
Career Touchdown Passes: **192**

Quenton Nelson

In nearly every circumstance, the word *little* doesn't apply to Indianapolis Colts guard Quenton Nelson—and never did. After all, he entered the world at a robust 10 pounds, 10 ounces. In his Pop Warner football days in Holmdel, New Jersey, he had to play two grades up until he reached high school. Nowadays, the sixth pick of the 2018 NFL draft stands 6'5" and weighs 330 pounds.

No, little and Quenton Nelson don't really fit—except in one specific instance. He has three older siblings, which means he will forever be their little brother. And it is a fact of life that little brothers, regardless of their physical stature, get picked on. In the Nelson household, Quenton's primary antagonist was Connor, who is six years Quenton's senior. Horseplay between the two ultracompetitive brothers was just a normal part of their daily lives. Well, at least until Quenton turned 14.

Few people would use *little* to describe Connor either. At the age of 20, the elder Nelson was 6'2", weighed 240 pounds, and played linebacker at Villanova. But by then, Connor's baby brother was about the same size. Home for Easter break that year, Connor tried to renew their sibling rivalry, but the status quo had changed. Nobody beat up on Quenton anymore, something big brother had to learn the hard way.

Still, all of those years being picked on had helped the younger brother develop a nasty dispo-sition on the football field. And excelling at offensive guard—perhaps the least glamorous position in football—requires a bit of nastiness. Quenton Nelson is known as a "block finisher," which means he doesn't let up until, as his father Craig puts it, he hears the echo of the whistle.

To be blunt, guard isn't the most highly coveted position on a football team. In fact, leading up to the 2018 draft, it had been 34 years since the Colts selected one in the first round. However, many scouts considered the unanimous All-American out of Notre Dame the most gifted player in the entire draft regardless of position.

So far, Nelson has lived up to—if not exceeded—expectations. He has made the Pro Bowl in each of his five NFL seasons, and he has been named a first-team All-Pro three times, including after his rookie season. Indeed, this little bro has some big game.

Position: **Guard**
Hometown: **Holmdel, NJ**
Born: **Mar. 19, 1996**
Height: **6'5"**
Weight: **330 lb.**
Team: **Indianapolis Colts**
Fact: **Five-Time Pro Bowler**

Micah Parsons

Dallas Cowboys linebacker Micah Parsons hates losing and always has—though these days he rarely does. Growing up in Harrisburg, Pennsylvania, he would get angry whenever his two older siblings would beat him in basketball.

He hated losing so much that he would go to great lengths to make sure it didn't happen. Once, a friend beat him badly at chess. Afterward, Micah downloaded some apps, studied different strategies, and then requested a rematch. He won. Another time, a friend beat him twice in a row in bowling. So Micah returned to the bowling alley to practice, even getting tips from the manager, who recommended that Micah switch to a heavier ball and taught Micah how to achieve consistent spin. After many hours of practicing, he won that rematch, too. Now, he owns eight balls, has a high score of 277, and aspires to be a professional bowler one day.

Micah didn't have the stablest of childhoods. His mom Sherese worked three jobs to support her three children. Micah moved five times in his youth, as his parents sought a safe place to raise their family. His father Terrence Sr. insisted his children play sports year-round, afraid of what trouble idleness could bring. Micah's first interest was wrestling. Terrence would drive Micah all over the country for tournaments, funded in part by Sherese cooking and selling meals to neighbors. Micah won national championships in youth wrestling.

But it was on the gridiron where he really made a name for himself. He began high school at Central Dauphin High, and after the fourth game of his freshman year, Pennsylvania State University offered him a scholarship. The five-star prospect, who eventually transferred to Harrisburg High School, was named the National Defensive Player of the Year at the U.S. Army All-American Bowl as a senior.

He decided to play college ball at Penn State. Although he started only one game as a freshman, he led the team in total tackles, becoming the first freshman in school history to do that. He was an All-American as a sophomore in 2019, but he sat out the 2020 season because of the COVID-19 pandemic. That didn't stop him from being the 12th overall pick of the 2021 NFL draft. It also didn't stop him from graduating, as Parsons completed his degree in criminology in three years. That's not bad for someone who had to repeat seventh grade because he wasn't taking his academics seriously at the time.

Being held back a year forced Parsons to reflect on what's important in life, and it instilled in him a deep desire to never fail again. So far, he has been a giant success for the Cowboys, winning Defensive Rookie of the Year in 2021 after compiling 13 sacks. In 2022, he racked up another 13.5 sacks en route to being named a first team All-Pro for the second straight year. For someone who hates losing, it's a good thing Micah Parsons so often wins.

Position: **Linebacker**
Hometown: **Harrisburg, PA**
Born: **May 26, 1999**
Height: **6'3"**
Weight: **245 lb.**
Team: **Dallas Cowboys**
Career Sacks: **26.5**

Roquan Smith

When the newly hired football coach of Macon County (Georgia) High School first caught a glimpse of Roquan Smith, the future NFL All-Pro linebacker for the Baltimore Ravens was playing basketball. Larry Harold knew instantly from watching Roquan that he was born to play football. Now all he needed to do was persuade the student, who had his heart set on the hardwood.

Harold asked for one year of football from Roquan, one year to show the freshman his future lay on the gridiron. Roquan relented, and Harold got to work. The first thing the coach did was give Roquan a new position, switching him from defensive end to middle linebacker. An offensive-minded coach, Harold hated playing against athletic linebackers who could make plays sideline to sideline. At defensive end, Roquan had been relegated to one side of the field, and offenses could just run the opposite direction. As a middle linebacker, Roquan could make his presence felt every play.

And that's exactly what he did. Following Roquan's sophomore year, MCHS defensive coordinator Kurt Williams put together a highlight tape of him, and Harold sent it to dozens of colleges. Before long, scholarship offers began to pour in from top programs around the country. UCLA was the first, then Mississippi. It turned out Harold was right after all: Roquan Smith was a football player, and one with big enough game to put his tiny community on the map.

Smith is from Marshallville, Georgia, a town so small it doesn't even have a single stoplight. His high school was located in Montezuma, itself a town shy of 3,500 people. Yet the biggest names in college football—Kevin Sumlin, Mark Richt, Jim Harbaugh, etc.—made the trek to try and lure Roquan to their respective schools. Roquan originally committed to UCLA, but a coaching change led him to reconsider. He eventually signed with Georgia.

As a junior, the 6'1", 232-pound dynamo led the Bulldogs to the national championship game, was named the Southeastern Conference's Defensive Player of the Year, was a first team All-American, and won the Butkus Award, which goes to the best linebacker in the nation. With nothing left to prove, Smith declared for the 2018 NFL draft, where the Chicago Bears selected him with the eighth overall pick.

Since then, no player in the league has had as many solo tackles as Smith, who was traded to the Ravens in the middle of the 2022 season following a contract dispute with Chicago. An economics major at Georgia, Smith has never hired an agent and represents himself in all negotiations. He has done all right for himself, inking a five-year, $100 million extension with Baltimore toward the end of last season. Not bad for a basketball player from small-town Georgia.

Position: **Inside Linebacker**
Hometown: **Marshallville, GA**
Born: **Apr. 8, 1997**
Height: **6'1"**
Weight: **232 lb.**
Team: **Baltimore Ravens**
Career Tackles: **693**

Justin Tucker

It all started with a tree–an oak tree, to be specific. This particular oak tree happened to grow in the backyard of Paul and Michelle Tucker in Austin, Texas, and its trunk split into a Y shape about six feet above the ground. It was at this tree that the Tuckers' 11-year-old son Justin would practice kicking footballs. In other words, this tree was Justin Tucker's first set of uprights.

Entering the 2023 NFL season, Tucker is the most accurate field goal kicker in NFL history, connecting on an outstanding 90.5% of the kicks he's attempted since the Baltimore Ravens signed him as an undrafted free agent out of the University of Texas in 2012. As far as kickers go, Tucker was a sensation from the get-go. He played an integral role in the Ravens' march to a Super Bowl title his rookie year. In the divisional round against Denver, Tucker's clutch 47-yard field goal in double overtime gave Baltimore an upset victory. His 38-yard fourth-quarter field goal in the Ravens' Super Bowl matchup with the San Francisco 49ers turned out to be the difference in the game.

And, yet, it's fairly easy to imagine an alternate universe where the six-time Pro Bowler and five-time first-team All-Pro never played football at all. By Texas standards at least, Justin Tucker was late to the game. He started off playing soccer, where he showed off his strong right leg by routinely sailing the ball above the goal. When he expressed interest in switching to football in eighth grade, his parents were initially hesitant. But a family friend–none other than the stepmom of former NFL QB Drew Brees, who went to the same high school as Justin–convinced the Tuckers to allow Justin to make the transition.

Even so, upon entering Westlake High School, Justin also dreamed of pursuing music. He had taken up the trumpet as a kid and then taught himself how to play the guitar. He wanted to pursue both of his passions, and his football coach even agreed to let his kicker split time with the band. The band director, however, wasn't so generous and forced the young man to choose. Miffed by the band director's intransigence, Justin decided to put his musical aspirations on hold.

It was a temporary hiatus, as it turned out. After he started at the University of Texas as a broadcast journalism major, he soon concluded this was not the path for him. So Tucker took voice lessons and auditioned for and was accepted into the university's Butler School of Music. There, he learned to sing opera in English, Russian, Czech, Latin, Italian, French, German, and Spanish.

This multitalented superstar, whose game-winning 66-yard "you-gotta-see-it-to-believe it" field goal against the Detroit Lions in 2021 is still the longest field goal ever made in an NFL game, has put his singing ability to good use. In 2015, he helped Gallagher Services, a charity for intellectually disabled adults, raise about $100,000 by performing "Ave Maria" at the Catholic Charities Christmas Festival at the Baltimore Basilica.

Position: **Kicker**
Hometown: **Houston, TX**
Born: **Nov. 21, 1989**
Height: **6'1"**
Weight: **183 lb.**
Team: **Baltimore Ravens**
Career Field Goal Percentage: **90.5%**

Fred Warner

For San Francisco 49ers linebacker Fred Warner, it's all about the little things. And it always has been. As a child, he wouldn't go to bed until his mother Laura helped him pick up all of his toys. Still, Laura noticed that her son lacked focus and needed somewhere to direct his energy. So she began enrolling him in sports.

Young Fred didn't take to soccer or basketball or T-ball. But from the moment he stepped onto a football field, he fell in love. In third grade, when signing a classmate's yearbook, he informed the young girl that he liked her because she liked football.

While his size helped him excel as a youngster, he struggled early on in his career at Mission Hills High School in San Marcos, California. He didn't start until his junior year, and at the time his one and only scholarship offer came from New Mexico State. It was at that point that a Brigham Young University grad and member of the Ward's Church of Jesus Christ of Latter-day Saints intervened and convinced the BYU coaches to look at Fred's game film.

The coaches were duly impressed and invited Fred and his family to visit the campus. It instantly felt like home. Laura also encouraged her son to commit to the Cougars, though her motives may have been a bit different from Fred's. She hoped BYU would equip Fred with a strong spiritual foundation—and perhaps a wife.

While Warner didn't find a wife at BYU, he did establish himself as an NFL-caliber player. He arrived on campus brimming with confidence and established himself as a playmaker early on. At the same time, Warner always felt he could be doing more—to grow more studious, more health-conscious, more dedicated. Beyond just enjoying the game, Warner relished the process of becoming great, whether by studying film or hitting the weights.

At BYU, Warner played a special position the Cougars' coaches called a "flash" linebacker, which is sort of an outside linebacker-safety-nickelback hybrid. Though Warner excelled, the position was different from anything run in the NFL. As a result, scouts weren't sure if his game would translate to the professional level. He was too big to play safety, yet, at 235 pounds, smaller than the prototypical NFL linebacker.

That explains why 69 players were drafted ahead of him before the 49ers called Warner's name in the third round of the 2018 draft. San Francisco uncovered a gem. He became a day-one starter and has started every game of his career over the past five years save for the one he missed in 2021 because of a hamstring injury. In 2022, he made his second Pro Bowl and was named a first-team All-Pro for the second time. For Warner, focusing on the small things has paid big dividends.

Position: **Outside Linebacker**
Hometown: **San Marcos, CA**
Born: **Nov. 19, 1996**
Height: **6'3"**
Weight: **230 lb.**
Team: **San Francisco 49ers**
Career Tackles: **634**

TJ Watt

Trent Jordan Watt was going into his third year at the University of Wisconsin, but he was starting from ground zero. The future Pittsburgh Steelers All-Pro outside linebacker hadn't played a single down his first two collegiate seasons because of a series of knee injuries. Then, in the summer of 2015, he received notice that head coach Paul Chryst wanted to move him from tight end to outside linebacker–a rather drastic change. In other words, TJ Watt had work to do.

It's a good thing, then, that the Watt family is known for a strong work ethic. That quality begins with TJ's parents, John and Connie Watt, neither of whom went to college. John spent more than a quarter of a century as a firefighter at the Waukesha (Wisconsin) Fire Department. Connie began her career as a secretary at a building inspection company but retired as its vice president. Every ounce of their hard work was necessary, too, because of the type of sons they were raising.

TJ is John and Connie's youngest child. He stands 6'4" and weighs 252 pounds. Even so, Connie would refer to him as her "peanut" because he was her tiniest baby. His oldest brother JJ retired from the NFL following the 2022 season after putting together what was surely a Hall of Fame career as a defensive lineman. His middle brother Derek is also TJ's teammate, as he plays fullback for the Steelers.

At one point, the Watts were routinely going through eight gallons of milk per week, and Connie was spending between $800 and $1,000 per month on groceries. Perhaps that explains why John angered TJ by making him quit his first love– hockey–in part because it was just too expensive.

So he turned his focus toward two things: shot put and football. In 2013, as a senior at Pewaukee High School, TJ won a state championship in the shot put, breaking the school record held by JJ, who himself had broken the record John set in 1980.

On the gridiron, TJ played, and excelled, at linebacker, tight end, quarterback, and punter. Even so, he wasn't considered a can't-miss recruit. ESPN rated TJ as the 28th best tight end in his class. Like his brothers before him, TJ signed with Wisconsin, eager to prove he was more than just JJ's baby brother. Instead, beset by injuries, he languished, at one point even asking his father how to become a firefighter. His fortunes began to change, though, when his position did.

He started that 2015 season almost like a freshman, having to learn the basics of outside linebacker. Fresh off knee surgery and in an unfamiliar place on the field, he was brought along slowly by the coaches. But he proved a quick learner–having an NFL superstar sibling to offer tips and insights didn't hurt. By 2016 the youngest Watt was playing at an All-American level. That year, he recorded 11.5 sacks though he felt he was barely scratching the surface of his potential.

NFL scouts noticed, and the Steelers selected Watt with the 30th overall pick of the 2017 draft. He went to the Pro Bowl in 2018 and was named a first team All-Pro three consecutive seasons, from 2019 to 2021. In 2021, he tied the NFL record by sacking the quarterback 22.5 times– despite missing two games. That season, he was named Defensive Player of the Year. If he keeps playing at this level, he may one day follow JJ straight to the Hall of Fame.

Position: **Outside Linebacker**
Hometown: **Pewaukee, WI**
Born: **Oct. 11, 1994**
Height: **6'4"**
Weight: **252 lb.**
Team: **Pittsburgh Steelers**
Career Sacks: **77.5**

Quinnen Williams

Like many NFL players, New York Jets defensive tackle Quinnen Williams has several tattoos inked on his skin. But the 6'3", 303-pound budding superstar, whose breakout 2022 season culminated with him being named to his first Pro Bowl while earning first-team All-Pro honors, may be the only player with one that features pink stars across his massive chest.

That particular tattoo carries great significance for Williams, though he likely wishes it's one he never had to get. It honors his mother Marquischa, who tragically passed away from breast cancer on August 10, 2010, at the age of 37. Quinnen, who of his three siblings was considered closest to Marquischa, was 12 years old and devastated by this loss.

Marquischa Henderson Williams, like her mother before her, was an elementary school teacher with a magnetic personality, sunny disposition, and a smile that could light up any room. Each of those traits are shared by Quinnen, Marquischa's second-oldest child. The pair was inseparable. They would cook and shop together, and Quinnen would even help her grade her students' homework.

Providentially, Marquischa left behind a tight-knit family that leaned on each other to get through the unspeakable loss. Quinnen's father Quincy Williams Sr. asked each of his four children to pick out a specialty to help keep the family running. Quinnen chose to become the family chef, and in high school he would wake up at 5 a.m. to work out before whipping up breakfast for everyone else.

Quinnen also kept himself busy with football. He attended Wenonah High School in Birmingham, Alabama, where he played with his older brother Quincy Jr., himself a star linebacker who played college ball at Murray State. As for Quinnen, he became a highly touted prospect and decided to sign with the college football powerhouse University of Alabama. He helped the Crimson Tide win a national title in 2017, won the Outland Trophy as the best interior lineman in the country in 2018, and was selected third overall in the 2019 NFL draft.

Williams's football career got even more surreal when the Jets signed Quincy Jr. prior to the 2021 season. The two brothers now start on the same defense, and they made history on October 3 of that year when they both sacked Tennessee QB Ryan Tannehill, marking the first time brothers recorded sacks in the same game for the same team.

For Quinnen Williams, life—and now football itself—is truly a family affair.

Position: **Defensive Lineman**
Hometown: **Birmingham, AL**
Born: **Dec. 5, 1997**
Height: **6'3"**
Weight: **303 lb.**
Team: **New York Jets**
Career Sacks: **27.5**

Trent Williams

NFL commissioner Robert Goodell strode to the podium at Radio City Music Hall in New York City on the evening of April 22, 2010, to announce the next selection in that year's draft. "With the fourth pick of the 2010 NFL draft," he said, "Washington . . . select[s] Trent 'Silverback' Williams."

Nobody could recall the often straight-laced Goodell ever using a player's nickname during the draft, but the name came up in a predraft meeting between the commissioner and the talented offensive tackle from the University of Oklahoma. It must have left quite the impression, and it's not difficult to see why.

At 6'5", 320 pounds, and freakishly athletic for his size, Williams attacked the game of football with ferocity, and his college teammates bestowed on him a nickname to honor that. Williams, for his part, has embraced the name, even getting a massive tattoo of a silverback gorilla on his back. He also has brought that same ferocity with him to the NFL, quickly establishing himself as one of the great offensive linemen of this—or any—generation. The Longview, Texas, native has made 10 Pro Bowl teams in his 12-year career to go along with two first-team All-Pro selections.

But even the most imposing players aren't invincible, and Williams is lucky to be alive.

In 2013, Williams discovered a lump on his head. Washington's doctors assured him at the time it was likely a harmless cyst. By 2018, though, the growth had gotten bigger and more had appeared. Concerned, Williams requested that a specialist look at it as soon as possible. Following the 2018 season, he prepared to undergo what he understood to be a simple procedure to extract the growth. Instead, at 30 years old, he was blindsided with grave news: The cyst was actually a tumor, a rare and terminal cancer called dermatofibrosarcoma protuberans that develops deep in the skin and was inching toward his brain.

At first, Williams worried most about his career. The situation, though, was much more dire. His doctor told him to get his affairs in order and recommended he spend as much time as possible with his two daughters Micah and Makayla, who were nine and five at the time and unaware of their dad's condition.

In February 2019, Williams underwent the first of several scalp reconstruction procedures, where it was discovered the cancer had not fully spread through his skull as was feared. Miraculously, his doctors successfully removed the tumor.

The ordeal caused a rift between Williams and the Washington organization, which traded their superstar to the San Francisco 49ers in 2020. With a new lease on life and football, Williams has picked up right where he left off. For the 2021 season, Pro Football Focus gave Williams an overall grade of 98.3, the highest-ever grade given to any player in any season. Not bad for someone who just a couple of years ago thought his time was up.

Position: **Tackle**
Hometown: **Longview, TX**
Born: **July 19, 1988**
Height: **6'5"**
Weight: **320 lb.**
Team: **San Francisco 49ers**
Fact: **10-time Pro Bowler**

Feb. 12, 2023: Jason Kelce (62) gets ready to snap the ball during Super Bowl LVII between the Chiefs and Eagles.